The Collector's Series / Volume 6

Keys to Successful
Baking

by Diane Phillips

AMERICAN
★COOKING★
GUILD

Boynton Beach, Florida

Dedication
To my family: to my mother for her inspiration and for being such a
good teacher; to Chuck for his encouragement; to Carrie and Ryan
who are my best helpers in the kitchen and the most honest tasters!
Also, to my friends and students, whose encouragement and
friendship have been invaluable.

Acknowledgments
—Cover Design and Layout by Pearl & Associates, Inc.
—Cover Photo by Burwell and Burwell
—Typesetting & Layout by Pearl and Associates, Inc.

Revised Edition 1997
Copyright © 1984 by Diane Phillips
All rights reserved.
Printed in U.S.A.
ISBN 0-942320-11-5

More...Quick Recipes for Creative Cooking!
The American Cooking Guild's *Collector's Series* includes over 30 popular
cooking topics such as Barbeque, Breakfast & Brunches, Chicken,
Cookies, Hors d' Oeuvres, Seafood, Tea, Coffee, Pasta, Pizza, Salads,
Italian and many more. Each book contains more than 50 selected recipes.
For a catalog of these and many other full sized cookbooks, send $1 to the
address below and a coupon will be included for $1 off your first order.

Cookbooks Make Great Premiums!
The American Cooking Guild has been the premier publisher of private
label and custom cookbooks since 1981. Retailers, manufacturers, and food
companies have all chosen The American Cooking Guild to publish their
premium and promotional cookbooks. For further information on our
special market programs, please contact the address below.

The American Cooking Guild
3600-K South Congress Avenue
Boynton Beach, FL 33426

TABLE OF CONTENTS

Introduction 5
Guidelines to Insure Success in Baking 5
   Oven Temperature...5
   Flours...5
   Butter and Shortening...6
   Nuts 6
   Chocolate and Cocoa 6
   Food Processor 6
   Measurements 7
   Baking Pans 7
Muffins 8
   Zucchini Muffins 8
   The Ultimate Bran Muffin 9
   Blueberry Muffins...10
   Date Nut Muffins..10
Breads 11
   Dilly Bread..12
   Honey Whole Wheat Bread 13
   All American White Bread 14
   Banana Bread...15
   Strawberry Bread..16
   French Baguettes...17
Cookies & Croissants 18
   Macadamia Coconut Cookies 18
   Thimble Cookies 19
   Whole Wheat Oatmeal Cookies 20
   Chocolate Dipped Shortbread Cookies.........................21
   Pecan Puff Cookies...21
   Croissants..22
   Whole Wheat Honey Croissants 24
Oven Pancakes 25
   Dutch Baby Pancakes..25
   Apple Oven Pancakes..25
Cheesecakes 26
   Pumpkin Cheesecake 26
   Amaretto Cheesecake...27
   The World's Best Cheesecake 28
   Chocolate Cheesecake..29
   Marble Cheesecake...30
Bundt & Tube Cakes 31
   Apple Pecan Cake 31

Sour Cream Coffee Cake 32
Grandmother's Sour Cream and Walnut Cake.............................33
Blue Ribbon Pound Cake 34
Zucchini Chocolate Cake..35
Pizzas...36
Tomato Sauce for Pizza..36
Pizza Siciliana..37
Spinach Pizza 38
Whole Wheat Pizza 39
Pizza Napoletana..40
Popovers 41
Plain Popovers 41
Cheese Popovers...42
Herbed Popovers Stuffed With
    Creamed Chicken and Mushrooms...43
Dessert Popovers—Warmuth's, The Port Side 44
Quiches and Tarts 45
Sugar Cookie Crust for Fruit Tarts..45
Vegetarian Quiche 46
Asparagus and Ham Quiche 47
Crab Quiche...47
Kiwi and Strawberry Tart...48
Orange Tart..49
Almond Strawberry Tart 50
Pie Pans...51
Flaky Pastry for One Crust Pie...52
Flaky Pastry for Two Crust Pie...52
Whole Wheat Pastry for Two Crust Pie 53
Berry Pie..53
Pecan Pie 54
Lemon Meringue Pie...54
Mother's Toasted Coconut Custard Pie 55
Sinful Satin Pie 56
Apple Crumb Pie 57
More Baking Favorites..58
Brownies..58
Apple Pie Cake 59
Carrot Cake..60
Blueberry Crumb Coffee Cake 61
Cinnamon Pull-Apart Coffee Cake...62
Artichoke Bread Appetizer 63
Southern Corn Bread...64

INTRODUCTION

The aroma of something baking in the oven sends most of us back to childhood with memories of mother's or grandmother's pies, cookies and breads. Baking is probably one of the most satisfying tasks one can perform in a kitchen. What could be more delightful than biting into a freshly baked croissant that has just been taken from your oven?

Baking for some people is a mystery. They assume that pie crusts are too difficult, yeast breads are confusing (what if it doesn't rise?), and many are reluctant to bake because they don't know how to use their equipment. The secret to baking anything is to begin with the best ingredients, a good recipe, and the best equipment that you can afford. The recipes in this book are designed so that you will know what equipment and ingredients are needed before you begin. Each chapter will guide you in the use of equipment, and recommend certain types of cookware over others.

All of the recipes in this book have been tested many times to insure success, but as with any new recipes, follow them closely and do not substitute ingredients.

SOME GUIDELINES TO INSURE SUCCESS IN BAKING

Oven Temperature

Many ovens have a great temperature variance. Even though the dial on the oven reads 325º, your oven may be cooking at 225º or at 425º. I recommend a **Mercury Oven Thermometer** to test the temperature of your oven and that you use it whenever you use your oven. Make sure that you preheat your oven with the thermometer on the middle shelf and then adjust the oven dial accordingly. Keep the thermometer in the oven while you are baking to make sure that you are maintaining a constant temperature. The temperature of the item you are baking will affect your oven temperature.

Flours

There are many types of flour available in the supermarkets these days. From the hard wheat grown in the United States, we have bread and unbleached flours. These flours are used extensively in bread making because of their high gluten content. Gluten is a plant protein found in grains which, when combined with other ingredients, helps to raise and expand dough.

From the soft wheat, which has less gluten, we have cake flour and pastry flour. These flours are used in pastry making, cookies and cakes. Pastry flours have become more difficult to find, but can be simulated in a recipe by using 1/2 cake flour and 1/2 unbleached.

All-purpose flour is in the middle (on the gluten scale), and can be used for most baking without any problem. If space is a problem and you cannot store more than one type of flour in your cupboard, buy the all-purpose flour for your baking needs. Your breads may not rise as high as they would with a high gluten flour, but the results will still be good.

Many times flour will become infested with small weevils. You should always throw away any flour that has weevils, buy a fresh package and put 2–3 bay leaves into your flour in an airtight container. The bay leaves will not affect the taste of your flour.

Butter and Shortening
Most of the recipes in this book will call for the use of butter. Butter imparts a richer taste to most pies, cakes and cookies. If, for dietary reasons you prefer to use margarine, please check the recipe to see if you can substitute margarine.

In many instances the use of butter is essential and it cannot be substituted. Many cooks prefer unsalted butter for its freshness and flavor. In these recipes you may use either salted or unsalted butter. **Each stick of salted butter contains 1/2 teaspoon of salt, and you should adjust your recipes accordingly.**

When recipes call for "creaming the butter," you may find it easier if the butter is at room temperature.

When using shortening, buy a good grade of pure vegetable shortening, such as Crisco®.

Nuts
Nuts are a delicious addition to most baked goods. Nuts store well in the freezer and can be added to any recipe directly from the freezer.

Chocolate and Cocoa
When using chocolate in a recipe, make sure that it is thoroughly melted and cooled before it is added to any mixture, or you will end up with tiny chocolate chips in your batter. There are two types of cocoa for cooking on the market: 1) the Dutch process cocoa, which has been processed with alkali, and is less bitter, 2) plain process cocoa, such as Hershey's®, which has a more robust flavor.

Food Processor
The advent of the food processor has given new hope to those who feared baking. Pie crusts are made in 10 seconds, bread is kneaded in 40 seconds, cakes can be mixed and become as light and airy as those blended by hand. I have included food processor instructions for all the recipes in this book because the food processor is one appliance I would not be without. It is a great time-saver and actually improves your kitchen's efficiency. Many kitchen chores that once seemed to take forever, (such as kneading bread) are done in just seconds. If

you do plan to do any heavy duty mixing in your food processor, make sure that it has a 6 cup capacity and that the motor can withstand a heavy dough.

Measurements

Measurements in baking are perhaps one of the most crucial elements to ensure success with a recipe. Dry measuring cups do not measure the same amounts as a liquid measuring cup would. For example a 1 cup dry measure amounts to 1 cup and 3 tablespoons of liquid measure. Use the right types of measuring cups for all your cooking.

Baking Pans

The equipment you use will also determine how successful your baking will be. We are fortunate to have such a wide selection of bakeware available to us. At the present time there are many companies that are marketing black steel baking pans. If you can afford to purchase one of these pans, you are in for a treat. The black steel pans conduct the heat evenly to insure crisp bottoms for piecrust, even rising for cakes, and popovers that rise to great heights! If you use the black steel pans, please read the manufacturer's directions and reduce your oven heat by about 25° and reduce the baking time about 10–15 minutes.

If you are interested in other types of bakeware, glass conducts the heat well, and generally produces good results. It also calls for a reduction in oven temperature by 25° and a reduction in cooking time of 10–15 minutes. Nonstick bakeware is great because it is easy to clean, but it generally lacks the heavy duty quality that one looks for in good bakeware.

MUFFIN PANS

Muffins are delicious for breakfast, lunch and dinner. Muffins are easy to make, and bake quickly, so they can be made on the spur of the moment. Muffins also freeze beautifully, and can be reheated quickly for a light snack. Insulated steel or tin muffin pans are excellent to use for muffins. I prefer not to use the paper liners that are available to make muffins. The batter rises higher when the heat of the pan actually touches the batter.

Miniature muffin pans are wonderful for dainty little cakes, quiches, and muffins. They should always be greased thoroughly before filling. Any standard muffin recipe that makes 1 dozen standard-sized muffins will yield 36 miniature muffins.

ZUCCHINI MUFFINS

1/2	cup brown sugar
3/4	cup butter or margarine
3	eggs
1	cup plus 2 Tablespoons flour
1/2	teaspoon salt
1	teaspoon baking powder
1	teaspoon baking soda
1/2	teaspoon cinnamon
1	cup grated zucchini
1/2	cup chopped nuts

In a large mixing bowl, cream the sugar and butter. Add the eggs one at a time. Blend in flour, salt, baking powder, baking soda, and cinnamon. When mixture is smooth, blend in zucchini and nuts. Fill greased muffin tins 2/3 full. Bake at 350° for 15–20 minutes.

Yield: 12 muffins

FOOD PROCESSOR METHOD
With shredding blade, grate zucchini using medium pressure. Remove zucchini from the work bowl and insert steel knife. Process sugar and eggs until smooth. Add butter, salt, baking powder, soda and cinnamon. Process on and off about 4 times. Add flour and zucchini and process on and off until flour disappears. Fill muffin cups and bake as directed.

The Ultimate Bran Muffin

1	cup milk
1	cup 100% bran cereal (such as All-Bran®)
1	cup flour
1	tablespoon baking powder
3	tablespoons sugar
1/4	teaspoon salt
1	egg (beaten)
3	tablespoons melted butter
1	cup of pecan halves

Pour milk over bran in a large bowl. Let stand 5 minutes. Add remaining ingredients, except for pecans. Stir until well blended. Make Honey Glaze as directed below. In 12 muffin tins, place 1 heaping tablespoon of honey glaze and 3–4 pecan halves. Then add batter, filling 2/3 full. Bake at 400° for 15 minutes. Turn out of pans immediately.

Yield: 12 muffins

Honey Glaze

3/4	cup shortening
1	cup brown sugar
1	cup sugar
1/4	cup honey
1/2	cup water

Cream shortening and sugars until light, gradually beat in honey and water until well combined. (Mixture may appear curdled.) This makes enough for 3 batches of muffins and keeps refrigerated indefinitely.

Food Processor Method

With the steel knife in the work bowl, pour in bran, and cover with milk. Let stand 5 minutes. Add egg, butter, salt, sugar and baking powder. Process on and off 4–5 times. Add flour and process on and off, until flour disappears. Proceed as directed above.

BLUEBERRY MUFFINS

    2   cups sifted flour
    3   teaspoons baking powder
   1/3 cup sugar
   3/4 teaspoon salt
   3/4 cup milk
   1/4 cup melted shortening
    1   egg
    1   cup blueberries

Place flour, baking powder, sugar and salt in a large mixing bowl. Blend in milk, shortening and egg. Carefully fold in blueberries. Fill greased muffin tins 2/3 full. Sprinkle tops of muffins with sugar. Bake at 425° for 20–25 minutes.

Yield: 12 muffins

FOOD PROCESSOR METHOD
With steel knife in place, add egg, sugar, milk and shortening to work bowl. Process until well blended. Add baking powder, flour, and salt, and process until flour disappears into batter. Remove steel knife and carefully fold blueberries into batter. Bake as directed.

DATE NUT MUFFINS

    1   cup dates
   1 1/2 cups boiling water
    2   cups flour
   1/2   teaspoon baking soda
   1/2   cup sugar
   1/2   cup brown sugar
   1 1/2 teaspoon salt
   1/2   cup butter or margarine
   1/2   cup chopped nuts

Place dates in a bowl and cover with boiling water. Let stand for 2 hours. Drain dates, and save liquid. (You should have 1 1/2 cups.) Pit and chop dates. Cream butter and sugars together, add date water, and mix in dates, nuts, flour, soda and salt. Fill greased muffin tins 2/3 full and bake at 350° for 25 minutes. These are delicious served warm, with sweetened cream cheese.

Yield: 12 muffins

FOOD PROCESSOR METHOD
With steel knife in place, combine sugars, salt and date water and blend for 30 seconds. Add dates and nuts, and process until chopped. Add butter and process on and off 4–5 times. Add soda, salt and flour, and process until flour disappears. Pour into muffin tins and bake as directed.

BREAD PANS

Many of my students groan at the prospect of making bread, but I find it so satisfying and easy to make a loaf of bread. Yeast is not difficult to work with, but because it is a living organism, it must be handled with care. Whenever you use a package of yeast, dissolve it in lukewarm water (105°–115°) and add 1/2 teaspoon of sugar. Set yeast mixture aside for 5–8 minutes. (You can use this time to assemble the other ingredients.) At the end of the standing time, the yeast should be bubbling on the surface. This means that the yeast is still active and that you can proceed with your recipe. If your yeast is not bubbling, start over. It is better to start over now than to waste your other ingredients.

Many recipes for yeast breads call for letting the dough rise in a warm draft-free place. Whenever I begin to make a yeast dough, I preheat my oven to 200°, time the oven for three minutes, and turn the oven off. By the time the dough is ready to rise, the oven is at the perfect temperature (warm, but not hot) and the dough rises perfectly every time. Yeast has a long shelf life and I generally store mine in the refrigerator.

Bread pans are available in black steel, glass and aluminum. The black steel pans are the best choice. If you can afford to purchase one, you will have crisp crusts and evenly browned loaves. If you use the black steel pans, remember to reduce your cooking time and temperature according to the manufacturer's directions. There are also multi-loaf pans available, which are 4 loaf pans that are held together and can be used to bake 4 loaves at a time. If you plan to multiply any recipes, double the recipe, but do not triple or quadruple a recipe. For the best results with all bread recipes, use either a bread flour or unbleached flour.

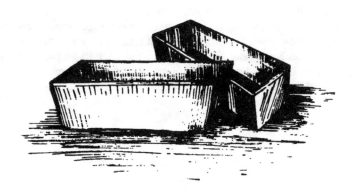

DILLY BREAD

2	packages active dry yeast
1/2	cup lukewarm water (105°–115°)
2	cups cottage cheese (room temperature)
2	eggs
2	tablespoons sugar
2	tablespoons minced onion
2	teaspoons salt
1/4	cup softened butter
1/2	teaspoon baking soda
1	tablespoon dill weed
5	cups flour

In a small measuring cup, combine the yeast, water and 2 tablespoons sugar. Set aside for 5 minutes.

In large bowl, combine cottage cheese, eggs, sugar, onion, salt, butter, soda and dill weed. Blend ingredients. Add yeast mixture, and stir until well combined. Add 3 cups of flour and stir until smooth. Add remaining flour 1/2 cup at a time, until dough is smooth and elastic.

Turn dough out onto floured board and knead until dough is elastic. Place in a greased mixing bowl and cover with a towel. Let rise for 1 hour.

Punch down and let rise 35–45 minutes or until doubled in bulk. Punch down, divide dough into 3 equal parts, and place in greased loaf pans. Let rise 30 minutes, or until dough begins to rise above sides of pan.

Brush loaves with melted butter, place in 350° oven and bake for 30–40 minutes.

Yield: 3 loaves

FOOD PROCESSOR METHOD

Place steel knife in work bowl of food processor. In small measuring cup, dissolve yeast in lukewarm water. Place cottage cheese, sugar, onion, salt, butter, soda, eggs, and dill weed in work bowl and process in 5–6 pulses. Add yeast mixture. Add all but 1/2 cup of flour and process until dough pulls away from sides of work bowl. Add remaining 1/2 cup of flour and process until flour is incorporated. Let rise according to instructions.

HONEY WHOLE WHEAT BREAD

This is a dense loaf. If you prefer a slightly lighter version, you may substitute equal portions of white flour for the whole wheat flour.

2	cups milk
3	tablespoons butter
1	tablespoon salt
1/2	cup honey
2	packages active dry yeast
1/3	cup lukewarm water (105°–115°)
2	tablespoons brown sugar
41/2–5	cups of whole wheat flour

Heat milk to simmering, add butter, salt and honey and pour into large mixing bowl. Dissolve yeast in warm water and add brown sugar. Let yeast stand for 5 minutes until it bubbles. Add yeast to milk mixture and stir until well combined. Add 2 cups of flour and stir until mixture is blended. Add rest of flour 1/2 cup at a time, until dough is smooth. Turn dough out onto well-floured board and knead until dough is smooth and elastic.

Place in a greased bowl and turn the dough so that the top is greased. Cover the bowl with a towel and let rise for 1 hour, or until it is doubled in bulk.

Punch dough down and let rise 45 minutes. Knead dough down and cut into 2 halves. Shape dough into 2 loaves.

Place in two greased loaf pans, cover and let rise 30 minutes or until dough begins to lift towel. Brush top of loaves with melted butter, and bake in a 375° oven for 30–40 minutes.

Yield: 2 loaves

FOOD PROCESSOR METHOD

Heat milk to simmering, add butter, salt and honey. Set aside. Dissolve yeast in water and add brown sugar. Let stand for 5 minutes to proof. With steel knife in place, put 3 cups of flour in work bowl, add yeast and milk mixtures, and process until smooth. Add 1 cup of flour and process until dough is elastic and smooth. Place in a greased bowl, covered with a towel and let rise for 1 hour.

Punch dough down and let rise 45 minutes. Knead dough down and cut into 2 halves. Shape into 2 loaves. Place in 2 greased loaf pans, cover and let rise 30 minutes until dough begins to lift towel. Brush tops of loaves with melted butter and bake at 375° for 30–40 minutes.

ALL AMERICAN WHITE BREAD

This versatile bread can be made into several variations. Try them all!

>2 *packages active dry yeast*
>1 *cup lukewarm milk (105º–115º)*
>2 *tablespoons sugar*
>4 *tablespoons butter*
>4 *cups flour*
>1 *teaspoon salt*

In 2 cup measure, dissolve yeast in lukewarm milk. Add sugar and set aside for 5–8 minutes. Pour yeast mixture into large mixing bowl, and add butter and flour 1 cup at a time until 3 1/2 cups of flour have been added. Turn onto a floured board and knead in remaining 1/2 cup flour until dough is smooth and elastic. Turn into a greased bowl and let rise until doubled in bulk (about 1 hour).

Punch down dough and let rise again for 45 minutes. Punch down again, and shape into a loaf. Let rise for 30–40 minutes. Bake in a preheated 350° oven for 30–40 minutes.

Yield: 1 loaf

FOOD PROCESSOR METHOD

In 2 cup measuring cup dissolve yeast in lukewarm milk and add sugar. Set aside for 5–8 minutes. With steel knife in place, place 3 1/2 cups of flour in work bowl. Add yeast mixture, salt and butter and process until mixture pulls away from sides of work bowl. Add remaining flour and process until flour is well combined. Proceed with rising instructions and bake as directed.

CHEESE BREAD

When adding flour, add 1/2 cups grated cheddar cheese to dough. Proceed as directed.

CINNAMON RAISIN BREAD

>1/4 *cup sugar mixed with 1 tablespoon cinnamon*
>1/2 *cup raisins*
>1 *tablespoon melted butter*

After the second rising, roll dough into a 12 x 18" rectangle. Brush dough with melted butter, sprinkle evenly with cinnamon sugar and raisins. Roll up dough from the short side and place in a greased loaf pan. Let rise for 30–40 minutes and bake as directed. This loaf may be iced with a simple confectioner's glaze of 1/2 cup confectioner's sugar blended with 2–3 tablespoons water. Drizzle over loaf while still warm.

Banana Bread

6	ripe bananas
2	cups sugar
2	eggs
1/2	cup melted butter
3	cups flour
2	teaspoons baking soda
2	teaspoons salt
1	cup chopped walnuts

Mash bananas with a fork. Stir in other ingredients in order given, until just blended. Do not overmix. Pour into two greased and floured 9 x 5" loaf pans and bake at 325° for 1 hour.

Yield: 2 loaves

Food Processor Method

With steel knife in place, place bananas and sugar into work bowl. Process with 4–5 on/off pulses. Add eggs and process until smooth. Pour in butter and nuts and process for 10 seconds. Add flour, soda and salt, and process in on/off bursts until flour disappears. Do not overmix. Bake as directed.

STRAWBERRY BREAD

1	cup strawberry puree (2 10-ounce packages frozen, or 2 pint baskets)
4	eggs
1	cup vegetable oil
3	cups flour
1¹/₂	cups sugar
2	teaspoons cinnamon
1	teaspoon baking soda
1	cup chopped nuts

In a large bowl, combine strawberry puree, eggs and oil. Blend in sugar, cinnamon and baking soda. Add flour and chopped nuts. Pour into two greased and floured 9 x 5" loaf pans. Bake 40–50 minutes at 350°. Cool completely before removing from pans.

This bread freezes beautifully and is delicious when served with sweetened cream cheese.

Yield: 2 loaves

FOOD PROCESSOR METHOD
With steel knife in place, puree strawberries, add eggs, oil and sugar. Process until smooth. Add cinnamon, soda, nuts and flour. Process until flour disappears. Pour into 2 greased and floured loaf pans. Bake 40–50 minutes at 350°.

SWEETENED CREAM CHEESE

1	package (8-ounce) cream cheese, softened
2	tablespoons honey
2	tablespoons cream or milk

With a wooden spoon, beat cream cheese until smooth, add honey and cream or milk until of spreading consistency.

FOOD PROCESSOR METHOD
Cut cream cheese into 1-inch pieces. Add honey and cream and process until smooth. Sweetened cream cheese will keep for 2 weeks in the refrigerator.

FRENCH BAGUETTES

1 1/2	cups lukewarm water (105º–115º)
3	packages active dry yeast
	pinch sugar
4 1/2	cups bread flour
1 1/2	teaspoons salt

In 2-cup measuring cup, dissolve yeast in lukewarm water with pinch of sugar. Set aside until yeast bubbles.

Place flour and salt in large mixing bowl. Gradually pour in yeast mixture and stir until flour is incorporated. Turn out onto a floured board and knead for 8–10 minutes. Let rise in a warm draft-free place for 1 1/2 hours.

Cut dough into 3 equal parts and form each part into a long narrow loaf (approximately 15" x 2"). Allow to rise another hour. Bake at 350º for 25–30 minutes, or until crust is a crisp golden brown. (To ensure a crisp crust, place a pie tin filled with 1 1/2 cups water on the lower rack in your oven while preheating. When loaves go into oven the steam will ensure a crisp crust.)

Yield: 3 baguettes

FOOD PROCESSOR METHOD

In measuring cup, combine yeast and sugar with lukewarm water. With steel blade in place, combine flour and salt in workbowl. With machine running, add yeast mixture and process until a smooth and elastic dough is formed. Proceed with rising instructions.

COOKIE SHEETS

COOKIES & CROISSANTS

Cookie sheets come in various sizes and are made of black baking steel or heavy tin or aluminum. The heavier the baking sheet, the more evenly it will conduct the heat and cook your baked goods. The newest type of baking sheet is one that sandwiches a cushion of air between two layers. These sheets, though an expensive initial investment, will ensure even cooking.

I like to line my cookie sheets with a sheet of aluminum foil (or parchment paper). This eliminates the need to grease the baking sheet and makes clean-up easy. (You can either throw away the foil, or clean it and reuse it.) When baking cookies, I will fill sheets of foil with formed cookies and slide the foil onto the cookie sheets for baking.

MACADAMIA COCONUT COOKIES

1	cup butter
1 1/2	cups sugar
2	eggs
1	teaspoon vanilla
1 3/4	cups all purpose flour
1 1/2	cups chopped macadamia nuts
2	cups shredded sweetened coconut

Cream butter and sugar until fluffy. Add eggs, one at a time, beating after each addition. Add vanilla. Add flour, nuts and coconut, and stir until blended. Drop by full, rounded teaspoons onto cookie sheet 1 1/2 inches apart. Bake at 350° for 10–12 minutes, until edges are golden brown.

Yield: 4–5 dozen cookies

FOOD PROCESSOR METHOD
With steel knife in place, process sugar and nuts 2–3 pulses. Add eggs, and process until blended. Add butter and vanilla, and process until smooth. Add flour and coconut and process until flour disappears. Bake as directed.

THIMBLE COOKIES

This recipe is adapted from one I received from a quilting friend at Christmas. They are a Christmas tradition at our house, with the children filling the thimble print with jam.

1	cup butter, softened to room temperature
1/2	cup sugar
1/4	cup brown sugar
1/4	teaspoon almond extract
2	egg yolks
2	cups flour
2	egg whites
2	cups chopped pecans or walnuts
	apricot or raspberry jam

In large mixing bowl, cream butter and sugar, add almond extract and egg yolks and stir until well blended. Add flour and beat until dough forms. Roll dough into 1" balls. Dip the balls into egg whites, then roll in chopped nuts.

Place cookies on a foil lined cookie sheet, and using a thimble or your finger, make an indentation in the center of each cookie. Fill with your choice of jam. Bake at 325° for 10–12 minutes. These cookies may be stored airtight, and they freeze well.

Yield: 3¹/₂ dozen cookies

FOOD PROCESSOR METHOD
With steel knife in place, process sugar, almond extract and egg yolks. Add butter and process until well blended. Add flour and process on and off until flour disappears. Proceed as directed.

Whole Wheat Oatmeal Cookies

1	cup butter or margarine
1	cup sugar
1	cup brown sugar
2	eggs
1	teaspoon vanilla
1 1/2	cups whole wheat flour
1/2	cup all purpose flour
1	teaspoon baking soda
1	teaspoon baking powder
2	cups quick cooking rolled oats
1	cup chopped nuts

In large bowl, cream butter and sugars until light and fluffy. Add eggs and vanilla and beat well. Add flours, soda, baking powder, oatmeal and nuts. Mix well, and drop by rounded teaspoonfuls onto cookie sheets that have been lined with aluminum foil.

Bake at 350° for 12–15 minutes. Cool on a rack and store airtight. These cookies have a caramel flavor and are a big hit with the children.

Yield: 4–5 dozen cookies

FOOD PROCESSOR METHOD
With steel knife in place, process eggs and sugar until blended. Add butter and vanilla. Add flour, soda, baking powder, oats and nuts and process until flour disappears. Bake as directed.

CHOCOLATE DIPPED SHORTBREAD COOKIES

  1   cup butter (do not use margarine)
 1/2   cup sugar
  2   cups flour
  1   teaspoon vanilla
  6   ounces chocolate chips, melted

Cream butter and sugar, add flour and vanilla. Pinch off 1/2-inch balls of dough, roll in granulated sugar and place on cookie sheet. Use the tines of a fork to flatten cookies. Bake at 350° for 12–15 minutes.

The edges of the cookies will be golden, and the inside will appear light in color. Remove from baking sheet, cool for 5–10 minutes on a rack and dip each cookie into melted chocolate, making one half of the cookie chocolate, and one half plain.

Yield: about 3 dozen cookies

FOOD PROCESSOR METHOD
Place steel knife in work bowl. Add flour and butter and process on and off until butter is the size of lima beans. Add sugar and vanilla and process until dough comes away from side of work bowl. Bake as directed.

PECAN PUFF COOKIES

 1/2   cup butter, softened to room temperature
  2   tablespoons sugar
  1   teaspoon vanilla
  1   cup finely chopped pecans
  1   cup flour

Cream butter and sugar until soft. Add vanilla, pecan pieces and flour, and beat until well combined. Roll dough into 1/2" to 1" balls. Place on greased cookie sheets and bake at 325° for 15 minutes.

While still warm, roll the balls in confectioner's sugar.

Yield: 30–40 cookies

FOOD PROCESSOR METHOD
With steel knife in place, grind pecans with sugar. Add flour, vanilla and butter, and process on and off until dough begins to form. Do not overprocess. Proceed as directed.

CROISSANTS

Croissants are an investment. They are an investment of your time and your ingredients. The croissant recipes that I have included in this book are streamlined from the traditional French methods, but still require about 4 hours of your time. There is nothing more satisfying than biting into a hot crispy croissant—especially when you have baked it! Filled croissants seem to be the rage right now, and I have included instructions for the proper folding of a filled croissant.

When baking your croissants, make sure that you are using a heavy baking sheet. (You will know if your baking sheet is not heavy, because it will buckle during cooking.) The black steel variety are by far the best and if you are fortunate enough to have one of these, your croissants will brown evenly. If you do not have heavy baking sheets, double or triple sheet the baking sheet you are using. Double sheeting is when you place another baking sheet under the baking sheet that you are using. This is not as convenient as using one black steel sheet, but will obtain similar results.

Because of the large proportion of butter used in croissants, the bottoms tend to burn if they are not watched closely and double-sheeted to protect them. Do not use margarine in your croissants. Margarine will produce a greasy, soggy croissant, which will disappoint you.

Croissants involve a number of foldings, called "turns" that make sure that there are layers of butter between the layers of dough. Make sure that you allow the dough to rest between the turns, or the dough will become tough and rubbery and you will be unable to roll it out. Croissants are fun to make, and a delicious "present" for your family to enjoy.

CROISSANTS

1	cup warm milk (about 70°)
1/4	cup melted butter
2	tablespoons sugar
1	package active dry yeast
2 1/4	cups bread flour, divided
3/4	cup plus 2 tablespoons cake flour
3/4	teaspoons salt
1	cup butter, flattened between waxed paper, into a 10" x 12" rectangle

In a large bowl, combine milk, melted butter, sugar and yeast. Set aside to proof yeast. After yeast has begun to bubble, beat in 1 1/4 cups bread flour to make a batter. then beat in remaining flour and salt. Wrap dough in plastic wrap and chill for 1 hour.

Roll dough out to a 12" x 15" rectangle, place butter on top of the rectangle. Fold up bottom third of rectangle onto the butter. Then fold top of the rectangle over the middle and bottom third of dough, folding as if it were a letter. This is called a turn. Turn dough 1/4 turn with fold on your left hand side. Roll out again and fold again in the same manner. Chill 1 hour. After 1 hour, roll out again, make one turn and chill 1 hour.

Roll dough out into a rectangle and trim the edges. Cut dough in half lengthwise, then into 3 equal parts crosswise. Roll each piece into a 5" square, cut into 2 triangles and flatten the short end of the triangle. Roll up from the short end of the triangle. Curve the edges and place on a foil lined baking sheet. Let rise in a warm place until doubled in bulk. Bake at 400° for 12 minutes. Reduce heat to 350° and bake an additional 5–7 minutes checking for even browning.

Croissants freeze well, either baked or unbaked and this recipe may be doubled easily.

Yield: 12 croissants

CHEESE CROISSANTS

During the first turn, sprinkle dough with 1 1/2 cups of shredded cheddar cheese (or your favorite cheese), then proceed as directed.

CHOCOLATE FILLED CROISSANTS

Coarsely chop your favorite chocolate bar, or use chocolate morsels to measure 3/4 cup. Instead of cutting triangles, cut squares in half. Place chocolate in center of dough, moisten outside edge of dough with water, and fold dough over chocolate. Let rise and bake as directed.

Whole Wheat Honey Croissants

3/4 cup warm milk (about 70°)
2 tablespoons honey
2 tablespoons melted butter
1 package active dry yeast
1/2 cup all purpose flour
2 1/4 cups whole wheat flour
1/2 teaspoon salt
1 cup butter, flattened between waxed paper,
into a 10" x 12" rectangle

In a measuring cup, combine milk, honey, melted butter and yeast. Set aside for 5–8 minutes. After yeast has begun to bubble, pour into a large bowl, and beat in flours and salt. Turn out onto a piece of plastic wrap and chill for 1 hour.

Roll dough out into a 12" x 15" rectangle and place butter on top of rectangle. Fold up bottom third of rectangle onto butter. Then fold top of rectangle over middle and bottom third of dough. Turn dough 1/4 turn with fold on your left hand side. This is called a turn. Make one more turn and chill dough for 1 hour.

Roll out dough again, and make one turn. Chill 1 hour.

Roll dough out into rectangle and trim edges, cut dough in half lengthwise, then into 3 equal parts crosswise. Divide each square into a triangle and roll from short end of triangle. Curve edges and place on a foil lined baking sheet. Let rise in a warm place until doubled in bulk. Bake at 375° for 12 minutes. Reduce heat to 350 and bake an additional 4–5 minutes.

Yield: 12 croissants

Oven Pancakes

Oven pancakes are easy and fun to serve. There are several pans on the market at the present time, but these pancakes can be made in a deep round pie plate. A food processor or blender makes these pancakes a snap to make, but they can also be mixed by hand. These are wonderful for Sunday morning breakfast.

Dutch Baby Pancakes

1/3	cup butter
4	eggs
1	cup milk
1	cup flour
3	tablespoons cinnamon sugar

In a deep pie plate, or oven pancake pan, melt butter in 425° oven. In blender or food processor, process eggs and milk. Add flour and blend until flour disappears. Pour batter into hot butter. Sprinkle with cinnamon sugar. Bake at 425° for 20–25 minutes, or until puffed and golden. Sprinkle top of pancake with lemon juice and sift powdered sugar over pancake. Serve with sausages, and maple syrup if desired.

Yield: 1 large pancake

Apple Oven Pancakes

1/4	cup butter
3	eggs
3/4	cup flour
3/4	cup milk
1/8	teaspoon nutmeg
1/2	cup chopped apples

Melt butter in an oven pancake pan, or other round baking dish, in a 425° oven. In a food processor or blender, process milk and eggs, add nutmeg and flour, and process or blend until flour is well combined. Pour into hot butter, top with apples. Bake at 425° for 15–20 minutes, or until puffed and golden.

Yield: 1 large pancake

Springform Pans

Springform pans are used primarily for making cheesecakes, which are elegant desserts that require very little effort on your part. Most cheesecakes taste better if they are allowed to "sit" for 12–24 hours. For these cheesecakes I recommend that you make them the day before you serve them. They should be refrigerated for at least 5–6 hours before serving.

Cheesecakes freeze beautifully, and can be thawed overnight in the refrigerator without any loss of texture or taste.

When using a springform pan for cheesecakes, let the cake cool completely to room temperature. Remove the sides of the pan, then remove the bottom of the pan by using a long, wide spatula to loosen the cake and slide it onto your serving plate. If you refrigerate the cheesecake with the bottom of the pan intact, the butter in the crust will get hard, and it will be next to impossible to remove the crust from the pan when serving.

All of these cheesecakes can be made with any of the crusts mentioned in the book. I find that the crumb crusts are lighter than pastry and add a little bit of texture to the cheesecake.

Pumpkin Cheesecake

Crust for 9" springform pan (graham cracker or pastry, whichever you prefer).

Filling

2	packages (8-ounce) cream cheese, softened
1/2	cup sugar
1/4	cup brown sugar
2	eggs
1	can (16-ounce) pumpkin puree
1	teaspoon cinnamon
1/4	teaspoon ginger
1/4	teaspoon nutmeg
2	teaspoons Gran Marnier (optional)

Place cream cheese in a large mixing bowl, add sugars and beat at medium speed until mixture is fluffy. Add eggs one at a time, beating well after each addition. Add pumpkin, spices and Gran Marnier, continuing to mix the ingredients thoroughly. Pour over the prepared crust and bake in 350° oven for 45 minutes to one hour or until a knife inserted in the center comes out clean.

Cool completely in pan. Release the sides, remove the bottom of pan and chill cheesecake thoroughly, before serving.

Yield: one 9-inch cheesecake

AMARETTO CHEESECAKE
CRUST

1¹/₂	cups of crushed amaretti macaroons
4	tablespoons butter, melted

Combine the amaretti crumbs with butter and press into the bottom and 1/4 inch up the sides of a 9-inch springform pan.

Note: Amaretti are crisp Italian cookies. They are sold in gourmet stores and in most Italian grocery stores. The brand that I use is called Amaretti di Saronno®, Lazzaroni & Co.

FILLING

3	packages (8-ounce) cream cheese,
1¹/₂	cups sugar
6	eggs
1	pint sour cream
1/4	cup Amaretto di Sarronno® liqueur

In large bowl of an electric mixer, beat cream cheese and sugar until light. Add eggs, one at a time, beating well after each addition. Add sour cream and amaretto, beating until mixture is smooth. Pour mixture onto crust and place in a preheated 350° oven for 1 hour and 15 minutes.

Remove from oven, and let cool completely at room temperature before removing the bottom and sides of pan.

Yield: one 9-inch cheesecake

THE WORLD'S BEST CHEESECAKE
CRUST

1   stick butter, melted
3   tablespoons sugar
2 1/2   cups graham cracker crumbs

Combine ingredients and press onto sides and bottom of a 9-inch springform pan. Set aside while making the filling.

FILLING

4   packages (8-ounce) of cream cheese
1 1/4   cups sugar
   grated rind and juice from one lemon
1/2   teaspoon vanilla
4   large eggs

Cream cream cheese and sugar. Gradually add lemon juice, rind and vanilla, beating until smooth. Add eggs, one at a time, beating thoroughly after each addition. Gently pour filling into crust. Bake at 375° for one hour.

Cake is done when top is golden and begins to show wide cracks. Cool cake in pan. Remove sides of pan when cake is thoroughly cooled. To remove bottom of pan, use a long wide spatula to separate the cake from the pan before you refrigerate.

Yield: one 9-inch cake

FOOD PROCESSOR METHOD
With steel knife in place, process eggs and sugar, vanilla, lemon juice and grated rind for 1 minute. Cut each package of cream cheese into 4 pieces. Add to work bowl. Process until smooth. Proceed as directed.

CHOCOLATE CHEESECAKE
CRUST

12   Oreo® cookies that have been crushed into crumbs
      (this should yield 1 1/4 cups)
1/4   cup melted butter

Combine crumbs and butter in a bowl and mix thoroughly. Press into the bottom of a 9-inch springform pan. Set aside while making the filling.

FILLING

3   packages (8-ounce) cream cheese, softened
1   cup sugar
1/2   cup sour cream
4   eggs
1   teaspoon vanilla
4   ounces of sweet chocolate, melted and cooled

In large bowl of an electric mixer, cream the cheese and sugar until light and fluffy. Beat in sour cream. Add eggs, one at a time, beating well after each addition. Add vanilla and melted chocolate, mixing until well combined. Pour into prepared crust and bake in 350° oven for 1 hour.

Cool completely and refrigerate. This cheesecake is dense and very rich. I like to serve it with raspberry puree and whipped cream.

Yield: one 9-inch cake

RASPBERRY PUREE

2   packages of frozen raspberries, defrosted, but not drained
1/2   cup sugar
1   teaspoon lemon juice

In a food processor fitted with a steel knife, puree raspberries. Add sugar and lemon juice and process for 10 seconds. Refrigerate until ready to use.

MARBLE CHEESECAKE

CRUST

1 1/4   cups graham cracker crumbs
2   tablespoons sugar
1/4   cup melted butter

Combine crumbs, sugar and butter and press gently into a 9-inch springform pan. Set aside while making filling.

FILLING

3   packages (8-ounce) cream cheese, softened
1   cup sugar
5   eggs
1   teaspoon vanilla
2   ounces unsweetened chocolate, melted and cooled

In a large bowl of an electric mixer, cream the cheese and sugar until light. Add eggs, one at a time, beating until well combined. Add vanilla, mixing until all the ingredients are thoroughly combined. Reserve 1 cup of batter and pour remaining batter gently over the prepared crust.

Mix the melted chocolate into the reserved one cup of batter and drop by tablespoons onto the batter in the pan. Taking the flat edge of a knife, make a swirling pattern through the batter. Do not overdo this procedure, or you will end up with a chocolate cheesecake.

Bake the cheesecake in a 350° oven for 45 minutes to one hour. Remove from oven and let cool completely before removing pan and refrigerate until ready to serve.

Yield: one 9-inch cake

BUNDT & TUBE PANS

Bundt and tube pans are used for large fancy cakes. These cakes make lovely centerpieces for buffets and festive parties.

A heavy black steel tube pan is the best choice for recipes calling for a tube pan. Bundt pans are usually made from heavy aluminum, and usually lined with teflon or other non-stick coating. A non-stick surface is recommended for ease of cleaning.

If you plan to use your food processor to mix your dough, make sure that it is a large capacity (6 cup) machine. Otherwise, divide the ingredients in half and mix your cake in 2 batches.

APPLE PECAN CAKE

1¹/₂	cups oil
1¹/₂	cups sugar
3	eggs
1	teaspoon vanilla
3	cups flour
1	teaspoon salt
1	teaspoon soda
1	teaspoon cinnamon
3	cups chopped apples
1	cup chopped pecans
¹/₂	cup raisins (optional)

In a large bowl, mix together oil, sugar, eggs and vanilla. Add flour, salt, soda and cinnamon. Blend well. Add apples, pecans and raisins. Pour into a greased and floured tube pan and bake at 350° for 1 hour and 25 minutes.

Yield: one cake, 10–12 servings

FOOD PROCESSOR METHOD
With the slicing blade in place, slice apples. Remove slicing blade, and set apples aside. With steel knife in place, process eggs, oil, sugar and vanilla. Add flour, soda, salt, cinnamon and process until flour disappears. Remove steel knife and gently fold in apples, nuts and raisins. Bake as directed.

SOUR CREAM COFFEE CAKE

STREUSEL TOPPING

1/3	cup brown sugar
1/4	cup white sugar
1	teaspoon cinnamon
1	cup chopped nuts

BATTER

1/2	cup butter or margarine
1/2	cup sugar
1/2	brown sugar
2	eggs
1	teaspoon vanilla
2	cups all-purpose flour
1	teaspoon baking powder
1	teaspoon baking soda
1/2	teaspoon salt
1	cup sour cream

Cream butter and sugars. Add eggs one at a time, and blend in vanilla. Add dry ingredients alternating with sour cream, stirring until smooth. Spread half of batter into a greased tube pan. Sprinkle half of streusel topping over batter. Top with rest of batter and sprinkle with remaining topping. Bake at 350° for 40 minutes.

Yield: one cake, 10–12 servings

FOOD PROCESSOR METHOD

With steel knife in place, add topping ingredients to work bowl. Process until nuts are chopped. Set aside. In same work bowl, process eggs, vanilla and sugars. Add butter and sour cream and process until smooth. Add flour, baking soda, baking powder and salt, and process until flour just disappears. Proceed as directed.

GRANDMOTHER'S SOUR CREAM AND WALNUT CAKE

My Grandmother made this cake as a treat for my Grandfather. It is a moist and delicious cake, that gets better after a few days.

1	cup butter
2	cups sugar
6	eggs
3	cups flour
1/2	teaspoon baking soda
1/2	teaspoon salt
1	cup sour cream
3	cups coarsely chopped walnuts
2	teaspoons vanilla

In large bowl of an electric mixer, cream butter and sugar. Add eggs, one at a time and blend well. Add dry ingredients alternately with sour cream. Add walnuts and vanilla. Pour into greased and floured tube pan. Bake at 350° for 1 hour and 10 minutes.

Yield: one cake, 10–12 servings

FOOD PROCESSOR METHOD
With steel knife in place, process sugar, vanilla and eggs. Add walnuts and process on and off until walnuts are chopped. Add butter and sour cream and process until smooth. Add dry ingredients and process until flour disappears. Pour into prepared pan and bake as directed.

BLUE RIBBON POUND CAKE

This pound cake stays moist and delicious for a week. It is delicious when served with fresh fruits in season, especially strawberries or peaches.

1/2	cup butter
2	cups sugar
4	eggs
3	cups flour
1/2	teaspoon baking soda
1	cup buttermilk
1	teaspoon vanilla extract
1	teaspoon orange extract
1	teaspoon lemon extract

In a large mixing bowl, cream butter and sugar. Add eggs, one at a time. Add dry ingredients alternately with buttermilk and extracts. Blend until smooth.

Pour into a greased and floured tube or bundt pan. Bake at 350° for 1 hour. When cool, remove from pan and sift confectioner's sugar over cake.

Yield: one cake

FOOD PROCESSOR METHOD
With steel knife in place, process sugar and eggs, add buttermilk and butter and blend until smooth. Add extracts and process on and off 4–5 times. Add dry ingredients and pulse on and off until flour disappears. Pour into prepared tube pan and bake as directed.

ZUCCHINI CHOCOLATE CAKE

1/2	cup butter
13/4	cups sugar
1/2	cup oil
2	eggs
1	teaspoon vanilla
1/2	cup milk
4	tablespoons cocoa
21/2	cups flour
1/2	teaspoon baking powder
1	teaspoon baking soda
1	teaspoon salt
2	cups grated zucchini
1/2	cup chocolate chips

In large bowl of an electric mixer, cream butter and sugar. Add oil and eggs and beat well. Add vanilla and milk, stirring until smooth. Add dry ingredients and zucchini, beating until blended.

Pour into a greased and floured tube pan. Sprinkle chocolate chips over the top. Bake at 350° for 45–50 minutes. Cool in the pan for 30 minutes. Remove from pan, and cool completely.

This cake can be served plain, or powdered sugar can be sifted over the top when it is completely cool. This cake freezes well, and should be wrapped air tight and refrigerated when cooled.

Yield: one cake, 10–12 servings

FOOD PROCESSOR METHOD

With shredding disc in place, grate zucchini. Remove from work bowl and set aside. With steel knife in place, combine eggs, sugar and oil. Blend until smooth. Add vanilla and milk, and process 3–4 on and off pulses. Add butter and blend until smooth. Add dry ingredients and zucchini and pulse on and off until flour disappears. Pour into prepared pan and bake as directed.

PIZZA STONES OR PANS

We all have our favorite type of pizza. My family likes Sicilian style pizza with a thick crust, tomato sauce and a light topping of cheese. Neopolitan pizza has a thin crispy crust, with lots of cheese.

A crisp crust is essential for a good pizza. A pizza stone can help to ensure a crisp crust. The pizza is baked right on the stone, without a pan. A black steel baking sheet or pizza pan is also an alternative.

The advent of the food processor has made making your own pizza dough a breeze. It takes longer to proof the yeast than to mix the ingredients. Thin crust pizza requires one rising, then it can be formed, filled and baked. A thick crust pizza rises once, then is formed, and allowed to rise again before baking.

The variety of toppings for pizza are endless, so use your imagination.

TOMATO SAUCE FOR PIZZA

1	cup chopped onion (1 large onion)
1	clove garlic, crushed
1/4	cup oil
2	tablespoons chopped parsley
1/2	teaspoon dried basil, or 2 tablespoons fresh
4	cups chopped pear-shaped tomatoes (2 1-pound cans, drained)
	dash of nutmeg
2	tablespoons sugar
1 1/2	teaspoons salt
1/4	teaspoon pepper

In saucepan, sauté onion and garlic in oil until it is translucent. (Do not let it brown.) Add parsley and basil and tomatoes and cook until juices have boiled down and sauce is a thick consistency. Add nutmeg, sugar, salt and pepper, and with potato masher, mash any large tomato chunks that remain. Cook 3–5 minutes longer. This sauce may be used on pasta or pizza.

PIZZA SICILIANA

1	package active dry yeast
11/4	cup lukewarm water (105°–115°)
2	tablespoons olive oil
1	tablespoon sugar
3	cups bread or unbleached flour
2	teaspoons salt
3	cups tomato sauce (see page 36)
2	cups grated cheeses
1/4	teaspoon oregano
2	tablespoons olive oil

In small measuring cup, combine yeast in water with olive oil and sugar. Let stand for 5–8 minutes. Place flour and salt in large bowl and add yeast mixture. Beat mixture together until it forms a ball. Turn out onto a floured board and knead for about 8 minutes, until it is smooth and elastic. Place in greased bowl and let rise for 11/2 hours.

At the end of the rising time, divide dough in half and roll out into two 12-inch circles about 1/2 inch thick. Place on lightly greased and floured pans and let rise for 45 minutes.

Top with tomato sauce and cheeses of your choice. Sprinkle with 1/4 teaspoon of crushed oregano. Drizzle 2 tablespoons of olive oil evenly over both pizzas. Bake at 425° for 20–25 minutes.

Yield: two 12-inch pizzas

FOOD PROCESSOR METHOD

Proof yeast with water and sugar. With steel knife in place pour flour and salt into work bowl. Gradually add yeast mixture and process until dough is smooth and elastic. Place in a greased bowl and let rise one hour. Form and bake as directed.

SPINACH PIZZA

1   *package active dry yeast*
1   *cup lukewarm water (105º–115º)*
2   *tablespoons olive oil*
1/4 *teaspoon sugar*
2   *cups bleached or unbleached flour*
1/2 *teaspoon salt*
1   *package frozen chopped spinach (defrosted and well-drained)*
    Mushroom Topping (recipe follows)

Combine yeast with warm water, oil and sugar. Let stand 5–8 minutes. In large bowl, combine flour and salt, add yeast mixture and drained spinach. Blend to smooth. Turn out onto well floured board and knead 8–10 minutes, until smooth and elastic. Place in greased bowl and let rise 1 hour until doubled in bulk.

Roll out into a 12″ circle that is 1/2″ thick and let rise for 45 minutes. Top with Mushroom Topping and cheese. Bake at 375° for 30 minutes.

Yield: 1 pizza

FOOD PROCESSOR METHOD
Dough: Proof yeast in small measuring cup with water, sugar and oil. With steel knife in place, add flour, spinach and salt to work bowl. Add yeast mixture and process until smooth. Place in greased bowl and let rise 1 1/2 hours. Form and bake as directed.

MUSHROOM TOPPING

1   *pound fresh mushrooms, sliced*
2   *tablespoons butter*
1   *clove mashed garlic*
2   *tablespoons chopped parsley*
1/2 *cup pureed tomatoes*
1/2 *teaspoon salt*
1/8 *teaspoon pepper*
1/4 *cup dry white wine vermouth*
    dash nutmeg
1/4 *cup grated mozzarella cheese*
1/2 *cup grated parmesan cheese*

In large skillet, melt butter and sauté mushrooms, garlic and parsley until liquid begins to evaporate. Add tomato puree, seasonings and wine. Cook mixture over low heat until thick. (About 5 minutes.) Top spinach pizza with this mixture. Cover with grated cheese and bake as directed.

FOOD PROCESSOR

Topping: With slicing blade in place, slice mushrooms. Remove from work bowl and saute in butter. With shredding blade in place, grate mozzarella cheese, and set aside. With steel knife in place and the machine running, drop parmesan cheese into machine and run until cheese is grated. Set aside.

With steel knife in place, place garlic, tomatoes and parsley in work bowl and pulse on and off until chopped. Add parsley, tomatoes and garlic to mushrooms in skillet. Add seasonings and wine and cook until thickened. Top pizza and cover with reserved cheese. Bake as directed.

WHOLE WHEAT PIZZA

This crust is not an authentic pizza dough, but makes an interesting pizza for those who prefer whole wheat flour.

> 1   *package active dry yeast*
> 1/2 *cup lukewarm water (105°–115°)*
> 1/2 *teaspoon honey*
> 1   *tablespoon butter*
> 1 1/2 *cups whole wheat flour*
> 1   *teaspoon salt*

Combine yeast with water, honey and butter. Let stand 5–8 minutes. In large bowl, combine flour and salt, and add yeast mixture. Turn out onto a floured board and knead dough 7–10 minutes, until it is smooth and elastic. Let rise in a warm draft-free place for 1 1/2 hours.

Roll dough into a 12 inch circle 1/4–1/2 inch thick. Place on lightly greased and floured baking pan. Top with your favorite tomato sauce and cheeses. Bake at 375° for 30 minutes, until crust is golden.

Yield: one 12-inch pizza

FOOD PROCESSOR METHOD

Proof yeast with water, butter and honey. With steel knife in place, add flour and salt to work bowl. Pour in yeast mixture and process until dough is smooth and elastic. Place in greased and floured bowl and let rise for 1 1/2 hours. Roll and bake as directed.

Pizza Napoletana

1	package active dry yeast
1	cup lukewarm water (105º–115º)
1/4	teaspoon sugar
2	tablespoons olive oil
2 1/2	cups unbleached flour (or bread flour)
1/2	teaspoon salt
3	cups tomato sauce (see page 36)
1/2	pound of grated mozzarella, monterey jack or parmesan cheese (a mixture of all 3 is best)
1/4	teaspoon oregano

In a small measuring cup, combine yeast with water, sugar and olive oil. Let stand for 5–8 minutes. Pour yeast mixture into a large bowl and mix in flour and salt, until the dough holds together.

Turn dough out onto a floured board and knead for about 10 minutes until dough is smooth and elastic. Turn dough into a greased bowl and let rise for 1 hour, until doubled in bulk.

Cut dough in half and roll each half into a 12" circle about 1/4 inch thick. Place on lightly oiled and floured baking sheets and top with tomato sauce and your choice of cheeses. Sprinkle pizza with 1/4 teaspoon crushed oregano. Bake at 425º for 20–25 minutes, until crust is crisp and golden. If you do not have a heavy duty pan to bake your pizza on, slide another sheet underneath it, so that your crust will not burn.

Yield: two 12-inch pizzas

Food Processor Method

In small measuring cup, combine yeast with water and sugar. Set aside for 5–8 minutes.

With steel knife in place, pour flour and salt into work bowl. Once yeast has begun to bubble, pour mixture into work bowl and process until it forms a smooth elastic dough. Turn into greased bowl and let rise for 1 hour. Follow directions for rolling and baking.

POPOVER PANS

Popovers are a delight to eat. They are light and airy, crunchy and delicious. The secret to making good popovers is to make sure that the batter is cold and that the popover pan is hot. This way, the batter will rise to great heights and you will receive compliments for your delicious triumph! Be sure you bake your popovers long enough, or they will collapse quickly.

There are several popover pans that are available at the present time. I recommend the heavy black steel variety. This type of pan is generally more expensive, but the investment is well worth it, for the quality of your baked goods is only enhanced by the quality of the utensils that you use. When using black steel, remember that as a rule you should reduce your oven temperature 25° and reduce your baking time by about 10–15 minutes, depending upon your recipe. Other popover pans that are available are made of stoneware and individual tin cups sold as set of six.

PLAIN POPOVERS

2	cups flour
2	cups milk
1/2	teaspoon salt
6	eggs
6	tablespoons butter

Place flour in a large bowl. Gradually add milk, eggs and salt, beating until well blended. Refrigerate this mixture at least 2 hours, preferably overnight.

Place 1 teaspoon of butter in the bottom of each cup of a popover pan. Place the pan in a preheated 375° oven for 3–5 minutes, or until butter is melted and the cups are hot.

Remove the pan from the oven and fill each 3/4 full. Return the cups to the oven immediately and bake for 45–50 minutes. Do not open the oven door for the first 30 minutes of baking time. Remove from oven and serve immediately.

Yield: 12 popovers

FOOD PROCESSOR METHOD
With steel knife in place, add flour and salt to work bowl. Combine eggs and milk and with machine running, pour eggs and milk through feed tube and process until well blended. Proceed as directed.

CHEESE POPOVERS

Cheese popovers have a marvelous aroma and taste.

1 1/2	cups milk
5	teaspoons vegetable oil
3	eggs
1/4	teaspoon salt
1 1/4	cups all purpose flour
1/2	cup grated cheddar cheese (or your favorite cheese)

In a small bowl, combine milk, oil and eggs, stirring until well blended. Combine dry ingredients in large bowl and gradually stir in liquids, until well combined. Add cheese and stir again. Refrigerate batter at least 2 hours, or overnight.

Place 1 teaspoon of butter in each cup of a popover pan and place in a 425° oven for 3–5 minutes, or until butter is melted. Pour popover into baking cups and fill to top (with larger popover cups, fill only 3/4 full). Bake at 425° for 20 minutes, lower heat to 350° and bake for 30 minutes more.

Yield: 12 popovers

FOOD PROCESSOR METHOD
With steel knife in place, add flour and salt to work bowl. Combine eggs and milk and with machine running, pour eggs and milk through feed tube and process until well blended. Proceed as directed.

HERBED POPOVERS STUFFED WITH CREAMED CHICKEN AND MUSHROOMS

1	cup flour
1/4	teaspoon salt
1/8	teaspoon sage
1/8	teaspoon thyme
1	cup milk
3	eggs
3–4	tablespoons butter

In large bowl, combine flour, salt and seasonings. Gradually beat in milk and eggs until smooth. Set aside and refrigerate for 2 hours or overnight.

Place 1 teaspoon of butter in each cup of a popover pan and place in a preheated 400° oven for 3–5 minutes. Pour batter into each cup about 3/4 full. Bake in the preheated 400° oven for 15 minutes, lower oven temperature to 350° and bake an additional 30 minutes. Remove from oven, split the popovers and fill with creamed chicken and mushrooms.

CREAMED CHICKEN AND MUSHROOMS

1	pound sliced mushrooms
1/2	cup butter
1/2	cup flour
1	can (10-ounce) chicken broth
1	cup heavy cream
1/4	teaspoon salt
1/4	cup chopped parsley
2	cups cooked chicken, cut into bite size pieces
2	tablespoons sherry

Sauté mushrooms in butter until golden. Blend in flour and cook, stirring over medium heat for 1–2 minutes. Add broth slowly and whisk until smooth. Stir in cream, salt, parsley and chicken. Heat until mixture simmers. Remove from heat and add 2 Tablespoons sherry. Serve in split popovers.

Yield: 12 popovers, 6 servings

Dessert Popovers—Warmuth's, The Port Side

Warmuth's was a restaurant in Boston that served this is a dessert. What could be better than a hot fudge sundae in a hot popover?

2	*ounces of unsweetened chocolate*
1/4	*cup butter*
3/4	*cups sugar*
1/2	*cup evaporated milk*
1/2	*recipe plain popovers*
1	*quart vanilla or coffee ice cream*
	hot fudge sauce

Melt chocolate and butter together over low heat. Add sugar and stir in evaporated milk and continue to stir, until sauce is smooth and thick. This sauce will keep in refrigerator for 2 weeks. Reheat over hot water in a double boiler.

To Assemble the Dessert

Remove hot popovers from oven and remove top. Scoop 2–3 scoops of vanilla ice cream into popover and cover with hot fudge sauce. Replace top and garnish with whipped cream and shaved chocolate.

Yield: 6 servings

QUICHE & TART PANS

Pans that have a removable bottom are great for making quiches and tarts that will be served on a lovely platter. I like these pans because the pastry can be laid across the pans, eased into position and the rolling pin will roll over the dough, and cut off the excess dough without having to make a decorative edge.

Once the tart or quiche is baked, it can be removed from its pan, and set on a decorative plate. Fruit tarts are elegant when placed on a buffet table. Quiches can become the main course when filled with a hearty filling, such as rataouille or the vegetarian combination I have included. Don't be fooled. Real men do eat quiche! If you do not have a quiche pan with a removable bottom, a straight-sided cake pan, or pie tin is also acceptable.

SUGAR COOKIE CRUST FOR FRUIT TARTS

1/2	cup butter
1 1/4	cups all purpose flour
1/2	cup sugar
1	egg yolk
1	teaspoon ice water

With a pastry blender, cut butter into flour and sugar until the mixture is coarse. Gradually add yolk and water and toss to combine. Form into a ball, refrigerate 1/2 hour and roll out into a 10" circle.

FOOD PROCESSOR METHOD
With steel knife in place, process flour, sugar and butter with 4–5 on and off pulses. Add yolk and run machine for 30 seconds. With machine running, add water and continue to process until dough begins to form a ball. Refrigerate for 1/2 hour before rolling.

TO PREBAKE A PIE SHELL
Place pastry in a greased pie tin and prick pastry with a fork all over. Cut a square of aluminum foil 2" larger than your pie tin. Press it into place and fill the foil with dried beans, rice or aluminum pie weights. Bake pie shell for 13–15 minutes at 425°. Remove from oven, reduce heat to 375°, remove foil and weights, bake for an additional 5–7 minutes, watching to see if it browns too quickly or puffs up. (If your crust begins to puff up, pierce it with a skewer or toothpick.) Cool on a rack.

VEGETARIAN QUICHE

1	tablespoons butter
2	green onions, chopped
3/4	pound mushrooms, sliced
1	cup frozen chopped spinach, defrosted and squeezed dry
4	eggs
1 1/2	cups heavy cream
1/8	teaspoon nutmeg
1	unbaked 9" pastry shell (see page 52)
1/2	cup shredded swiss cheese
3	tablespoons grated parmesan cheese

In a skillet, melt the butter, add onions and mushrooms, and cook until most of the liquid is absorbed. Add spinach and cook until liquid is absorbed. Set aside. Beat eggs, cream and nutmeg. Stir in spinach mixture. Pour into pastry shell. Sprinkle with cheeses and bake at 350° for 30–40 minutes. Let stand 10 minutes before cutting.

Yield: 1 quiche, 6–8 servings

FOOD PROCESSOR METHOD
With slicing blade in place, stack mushrooms lengthwise and slice, using medium pressure. With shredding blade in place, shred cheeses. Cook mushrooms and spinach as directed. Place in unbaked pie shell. With steel knife in place, process cream, eggs and seasonings. Pour over spinach mixture and top with cheese. Bake as directed.

Asparagus and Ham Quiche

2	tablespoons butter
1	cup diced boiled ham
6	ounces of cooked asparagus
1	unbaked 9" pastry shell (see page 52)
4	eggs
1	cup whipping cream
1/4	teaspoon nutmeg
1 1/2	cups grated swiss cheese

Melt butter in a large skillet, add ham and toss until well coated. Add asparagus, and toss together to blend the flavors. Place ham and asparagus in unbaked pie shell. Combine eggs, whipping cream and nutmeg. Pour over ham and asparagus. Top with swiss cheese and bake at 350° for 40 minutes.

Yield: 1 quiche, 6–8 servings

Food Processor Method
With steel knife in place, dice ham, using on and off pulses. Remove from work bowl and saute in melted butter with asparagus. With shredding disc in place, grate cheese. Set aside. With steel knife in place, process eggs, cream and nutmeg. Place ham and asparagus in pie shell, top with egg and cream mixture and cover with swiss cheese.

Crab Quiche

3	eggs
1	cup whipping cream
1/4	cup chopped green onion
1	cup cooked crab meat, drained and with shell removed
1	unbaked 9" pie shell (see page 52)
1 1/2	cups grated swiss cheese

In a large bowl, beat eggs and cream. Add green onion and crab meat. Pour into unbaked pie shell and top with grated cheese. Bake at 375° for 45 minutes, until puffed and golden.

Food Processor Method
With shredding disc in place, grate cheese, and set aside. With steel knife in place, process eggs, cream and green onion. Place crab in unbaked pie shell, pour egg mixture over crab and top with grated cheese. Bake as directed.

KIWI AND STRAWBERRY TART

1	package (8 ounces) cream cheese
1	tablespoon Gran Marnier
1/2	cup sugar
1	prebaked sugar cookie crust (see page 45)
2	kiwi fruit, peeled and sliced 1/2 inch thick
1	cup whole strawberries
1/2	cup water
3/4	cup orange juice
2	tablespoons Gran Marnier
2	tablespoons cornstarch
3/4	cup sugar

Beat cream cheese and Gran Marnier until smooth, add sugar and beat again. Spread in cooled pie shell.

Wash strawberries and dry thoroughly on paper towels. Stand the strawberries in middle of tart, with pointed side up. Overlapping slides of kiwi, fill in outer portion of tart.

In a small saucepan, combine water, orange juice, Gran Marnier, cornstarch and sugar and bring to a boil. Stir constantly and boil for 1 minute. Remove from heat and cool. When cool, spread glaze over kiwi and strawberries. Chill for at least 2 hours. Serve cold.

Yield: 6–8 servings

FOOD PROCESSOR METHOD

With the slicing blade in place, slice kiwi fruit, using moderate pressure. Set aside, rinse work bowl and put steel knife in place. Add cream cheese, Gran Marnier and sugar in work bowl and process until smooth. Spread in cooled pastry shell and proceed as directed.

ORANGE TART

1 package (8-ounce) cream cheese
1 teaspoon orange extract
2 tablespoons milk
1 cup sugar
1 prebaked sugar cookie crust (see page 45)
3/4 cup water
1/4 cup lemon juice
3 tablespoons cornstarch
1 cup sugar
2 tablespoons rum
1 cup orange juice
8 seedless oranges

Beat cream cheese, extract, milk and sugar until smooth. Spread into cooled crust. Peel oranges and slice lengthwise in 1/2″ slices. Save any juice that accumulates from oranges.

In a saucepan, combine water, lemon juice, cornstarch, sugar and rum. Collect any orange juice that has accumulated from oranges. Add enough orange juice to measure 1 cup. Add orange juice to mixture in sauce pan and bring to a boil. Boil for 1 minute. Cool thoroughly.

Lay oranges on cream cheese, overlapping slightly. When glaze is cooled, spoon over oranges and chill thoroughly before serving.

Yield: 8–10 servings

FOOD PROCESSOR METHOD
With slicing disc in place, slice oranges, using moderate pressure. Set aside and save any juice that accumulates. With steel knife in place, process cream cheese, sugar and milk until smooth. Spread into cooled pie shell. Top with oranges. Prepare glaze and cool. Spoon glaze over oranges, chill before serving.

ALMOND STRAWBERRY TART

1   cup milk
3   egg yolks
1/3 cup sugar
2   tablespoons cornstarch
1   teaspoon almond extract
3   pint baskets of strawberries, washed and thoroughly dried
1   jar (10-ounce) strawberry jelly
1/4 cup sliced almonds
1/4 cup sifted powdered sugar
1   prebaked sugar cookie crust (see page 45)

In a saucepan, heat milk to boiling. Meanwhile whisk egg yolks and sugar together until thick. Gradually stir in cornstarch, continue whisking and add hot milk. Pour mixture into saucepan and bring to a boil for 1 minute. Remove from heat and add almond extract. Cool completely.

When pastry cream is cooled, spread into prepared crust. Place cleaned strawberries pointed side up on pastry cream. Melt strawberry jelly over low heat. Spoon jelly over each strawberry, until tart is entirely glazed. Garnish outside edge with sliced almonds. Sift powdered sugar over almonds and chill.

Yield: 8–10 servings

PIE PANS

There is nothing more impressive than a fresh baked pie with its flaky crust and delightful filling. Many of my students complain that their pie crusts are tough, or they fall apart before they can get them into the pie plate, or that their custard fillings are runny, and their meringue weeps. In this chapter, there are fool proof crusts and the fillings are easy and delicious.

A few things to remember when working with pastry crust. The fat used, (butter, margarine, or shortening) should always be cut into the flour, until it resembles coarse meal. The size of the fat should be about the size of a grain of rice or tiny peas. Ice water should always be added a tablespoon at a time to the fat and flour mixture, and then tossed until the mixture just holds together.

Always shape the dough into a ball, cover and chill for at least 30 minutes to rest. Using a minimum amount of four, flour both sides of the dough, the rolling pin and board. Always roll dough from the center out and do not turn dough over when rolling it out. If edges crack, pinch them together; if there is a hole in dough, patch it with a scrap. **Do not reroll pastry dough, or it will become tough.**

Pastry takes time, patience, and practice. Once the pie shell has been shaped and placed into the pie plate, place the pie in the freezer for 30 minutes to set the crust, and relax the dough. Then proceed with filling and baking instructions.

All shaped pie crusts can be frozen if they are wrapped air tight. All-purpose flour is the flour of choice when making pastry.

Pie plates or tins come in different, graduated sizes. The most common pie plates are 8, 9 and 10 inches. I like to use a glass pie plate. The crust becomes crisp and golden, and not soggy. Other pie tins are made of black steel and heavy tin. A 9" pie tin is a good size to purchase.

FLAKY PASTRY FOR ONE CRUST PIE

   1   *stick butter or margarine (or 1/2 cup shortening)*
1 1/2 *cups flour*
   1   *teaspoon salt*
 1/4 *cup ice water*

Cup butter into flour and salt. Add water a tablespoon at a time, and toss together until dough forms a ball. Chill 1/2 hour, and roll out.

Yield: one 9-inch pie shell

FOOD PROCESSOR METHOD
With steel knife in place, place flour and salt in work bowl. Cut butter into 1/2 inch pieces and drop on top of flour and salt mixture. Process mixture with 4–5 on and off bursts. With machine running, pour in water, gradually, until dough begins to pull away from sides of work bowl. **Do not let dough form a ball or it will be overprocessed and impossible to roll out.**

FLAKY PASTRY FOR A TWO CRUST PIE

 3/4 *cup plus 2 tablespoons shortening*
2 1/4 *cups flour*
   1   *teaspoon salt*
 1/3 *cup cold water*

With a pastry blender, or two knives cut shortening into flour and salt until shortening is the size of small peas. Sprinkle water (1 tablespoon at a time) over flour and shortening and toss together with your fingers until the mixture forms a ball. Cover dough with plastic wrap and refrigerate at least 1/2 hour. Divide dough in half and roll out.

Yield: two 9-inch pie shells

FOOD PROCESSOR METHOD
With steel knife in place, add flour and salt to work bowl. Drop shortening onto flour and process on and off 5–6 times. With machine running, gradually add ice water until dough begins to form a ball. Stop machine, turn dough out onto a piece of plastic wrap and refrigerate for 1/2 hour.

WHOLE WHEAT PASTRY FOR 2 CRUST PIE

2¹/₄ cups whole wheat flour
¹/₄ cup all purpose flour
¹/₄ teaspoon salt
³/₄ cup shortening
²/₃ cup ice water

In large bowl, combine flours and salt. Cut in shortening until it is the size of small peas. Add ice water 1 Tablespoon at a time, tossing mixture together, until it is well combined and forms a ball. This dough should be refrigerated for at least two hours before rolling.

FOOD PROCESSOR METHOD

With steel knife in place, add flours and salt to work bowl. Drop in shortening and process on and off 5–6 times until shortening is size of peas. With machine running, gradually add ice water until dough has begun to form. Remove from work bowl, wrap in plastic wrap and refrigerate for 2 hours before rolling into two pie shells.

BERRY PIE

whole wheat pastry for a double crust pie (recipe above)
1 package (16-ounce) frozen berries (blackberries, boysenberries or black raspberries) or 4 cups of fresh berries, washed
1¹/₄ cups sugar
3 tablespoons cornstarch
1¹/₂ tablespoons lemon juice
1¹/₂ tablespoons butter

If using frozen berries, place berries in a large bowl and toss with sugar, cornstarch and lemon juice. Set aside and allow berries to separate before placed into pie crust. (Do not allow berries to stick together when placed into pie shell.) If using fresh berries, toss with cornstarch, sugar and lemon juice and place into pie shell.

Place berries in prepared pie shell. Top berries with 2 tablespoons butter, that you have have cut into slivers. Place top crust on, seal edges and cut decorative slits into the top of crust. Bake pie at 400° for 15 minutes, reduce heat to 350° for 45–55 minutes.

Yield: one 9-inch pie

PECAN PIE

1 cup white corn syrup
1 cup dark brown sugar
1/4 teaspoon salt
1/2 cup melted butter
1 teaspoon vanilla
3 eggs
1 unbaked 9" pie shell (see page 52)
2 cups shelled pecan halves

Combine syrup, sugar, salt, butter, vanilla and eggs and mix well with a wire whisk. Pour into pastry shell and sprinkle with pecans. Bake at 350° for 45 minutes. Serve with vanilla ice cream.

Yield: one 9-inch pie

FOOD PROCESSOR METHOD
With steel knife in place, add eggs to work bowl with sugar, salt, butter and vanilla. Process until blended. Add corn syrup and process with on and off pulses until incorporated. Pour into pie shell, top with pecans and bake as directed.

LEMON MERINGUE PIE

1 baked 9" pie shell (see page 52)
6 tablespoons cornstarch
11/3 cups sugar
1/4 teaspoon salt
11/2 cups warm water
2 tablespoons butter or margarine
4 egg yolks
2 tablespoons grated lemon rind
1/3 cup lemon juice

In a 2-quart saucepan, mix cornstarch, sugar and salt, and gradually add water whisking slowly. Place over medium heat, and stir constantly until mixture becomes clear and boils for 2 minutes. Remove from heat, add butter and stir until it is melted.

In a small bowl, beat yolks and add a few tablespoons of hot mixture to yolks. Pour entire yolk mixture into hot cornstarch mixture, and stir to combine. Add lemon rind and lemon juice and whisk until smooth. Return to moderate heat and bring to a boil, stirring for 1 minute. Pour hot mixture into pie crust.

MERINGUE

    4   egg whites
        pinch of cream of tartar
  1/3   cup sugar

In small bowl of electric mixer, place egg whites, and beat on medium speed until foamy. Add cream of tartar, and beat at high speed until whites can hold a soft peak when beater is raised. Fold in sugar with a spatula, 2 Tablespoons at a time. When sugar is completely incorporated, whip the mixture again, until stiff.

With a large tablespoon, drop meringue around the outside of the pie. Spread it to seal the crust and cover the filling completely. Make sure crust is completely sealed, or your meringue will be runny. Bake pie at 400° for 5–7 minutes, or until meringue is a light golden color.

Yield: one 9-inch pie

MOTHER'S TOASTED COCONUT CUSTARD PIE

    1   9" pie shell, unbaked (see page 52)
    4   eggs, slightly beaten
  1/2   cup sugar
  1/2   teaspoon salt
    1   teaspoon vanilla
  1/4   teaspoon nutmeg
    2   cups milk, scalded
    1   cup shredded coconut, toasted to a golden brown

In a large bowl, beat eggs until light and lemon colored and add sugar gradually. Add salt, vanilla and nutmeg. Pour some hot milk into eggs, and then pour all of egg mixture into hot milk, blend well and add 1/2 cup of coconut to mixture.

Pour into pie shell and top with remaining coconut. Bake at 450° for 15 minutes, reduce heat to 325° and bake an additional 30 minutes.

Yield: one 9-inch pie

FOOD PROCESSOR METHOD
With steel knife in place, process eggs, sugar, salt, vanilla and nutmeg until blended. With machine running, gradually add hot milk in a slow stream until well combined. Add 1/2 cup coconut and process with 2–3 on and off bursts. Pour into pie shell, top with remaining coconut and bake as directed.

SINFUL SATIN PIE

Although the crust is the only part of this pie that is baked, it is a wonderfully devilish pie that you will love.

CRUST

3/4	cup graham cracker crumbs
1/2	cup ground toasted almonds (to toast almonds, place them on a cookie sheet in a 350° oven and toast until golden)
1/4	cup powdered sugar
1/4	cup melted butter

Combine ingredients and press into a 9" pie pan. Bake at 350° for 10 minutes. Remove from oven and let cool completely.

FILLING

2	eggs
3/4	cup sugar
1	tablespoon Kahlua liqueur
1/2	teaspoon vanilla
6	ounces of chocolate chips, melted and cooled
2	sticks of unsalted butter

In the large bowl of an electric mixer, beat eggs, sugar, Kahlua and vanilla until light. Add chocolate chips and blend. Beat in butter, one stick at a time, until mixture is smooth. Pour into cooled pie shell. Top with whipped cream topping.

WHIPPED CREAM TOPPING

2	cups whipping cream
1/4	cup confectioner's sugar
1	teaspoon powdered coffee

In the small bowl of an electric mixer, pour in cream, and powdered sugar. Beat until it begins to form peaks. Add coffee powder and beat until stiff peaks form. Use this whipped cream topping to top pie. Decorate with shaved chocolate, and serve cold.

This pie may be frozen without the topping. Thaw overnight in refrigerator and prepare topping 3–4 hours before serving.

Yield: one 9-inch pie

Food Processor
Crust: with steel knife in place, combine graham crackers, almonds, sugar and butter. Pulse on and off 4–5 times. Pour into pie pan and bake as directed.

Filling: with steel knife in place, process eggs, sugar, Kahlua and vanilla. Add melted chocolate and butter, and process until smooth. Pour into pie shell.

Topping: the topping can be made in the food processor, but will not be as light and airy. If you prefer to make it in the food processor, with steel knife in place, process cream, sugar and coffee powder until stiff. Top pie with filling.

Apple Crumb Pie

1	9" unbaked pastry shell (see page 52)
7	green cooking apples, peeled, cored and sliced
1/2	cup sugar
3/4	teaspoon ground cinnamon
6	tablespoons butter
3/4	cup flour
1/3	cup sugar

Prepare apples, place in a large bowl and toss with 1/2 cup sugar and 3/4 teaspoon cinnamon. Let stand and prepare crumb topping.

With a pastry blender, cut butter into flour until it is crumbly. Add sugar and toss together. Pour apples into prepared crust and top with crumb topping. Bake at 375° for 40 minutes. Cool before cutting and serve with vanilla ice cream.

Yield: one 9-inch pie

Food Processor Method
With slicing disc, slice apples; place in bowl with sugar and cinnamon. With steel knife in place, add flour to work bowl. Cut butter into 1/2" pieces and drop on top of flour. Add sugar to work bowl and process on and off until mixture is crumbly—do not overprocess or you will end up with a ball of dough! Place apples in pie crust and top with crumbs. Bake as directed.

SQUARE, ROUND & RECTANGULAR BAKING PANS

If I were left on a desert island with only one item to bake in, I would hope that it would be my 13" x 9" baking dish. A 13"·x 9" pan can be used to make cakes, deep dish pies, lasagne, bar cookies and quick breads. It is a good size for serving company and for your family. Square pans and round pans come in several sizes, and if you only want to buy one size, the 8" is probably the best.

Any of the recipes in this chapter for round and square pans can be doubled, and baked in a 13" x 9"" pan. Those for 13" x 9" pans can be halved to fit an 8" pan. Black steel and glass are best conductors of heat in this category, and are highly recommended. Make sure that whatever you buy does not rust, otherwise you will have problems later on.

The cornbread recipe that I have included can also be made in a cast iron skillet. If you are lucky enough to have one of these treasures, take good care of it by using it often. If you have an old cast iron skillet that needs some TLC, scour it well with soap and water, then clean it with steel wool or sand paper to remove the rust. When you have removed the rust, coat skillet with mineral oil (found in pharmacies) and bake at 325° for 20 minutes. At the end of the 20 minutes, recoat the pan and bake again for another 20 minutes. Recoat the pan again and bake an additional 20 minutes. Cool it thoroughly. Wipe it with a dry cloth and store. Always coat the skillet with mineral oil after cleaning.

BROWNIES

Everyone has their favorite brownie recipe, and I am no exception. These brownies are a chocolate lovers delight!

1	cup butter
2	cups sugar
4	eggs
1	cup cocoa
1	cup flour
1	cup chopped walnuts
1	cup chocolate chips

Cream butter and sugar together, add eggs, one at a time. Beat in cocoa, flour, walnuts and half of the chocolate chips. Spread into a greased and floured 13" x 9" pan. Top with remaining chocolate chips. Bake at 325° for 40–50 minutes. Cool completely before cutting.

Yield: 2 dozen brownies

FOOD PROCESSOR METHOD

With steel knife in place, process nuts with sugar. Add eggs and process until blended. Add butter and pulse on and off 4–5 times, until smooth. Add flour and cocoa and pulse on and off until flour disappears. Add half of chocolate chips and pulse on and off 2–3 times. Pour into prepared pan and top with remaining chocolate chips. Bake as directed.

APPLE PIE CAKE

6–8	*apples, peeled and sliced*
1	*teaspoon cinnamon*
1	*tablespoon sugar*
1	*teaspoon lemon juice*
3/4	*cup butter or margarine*
1	*cup flour*
1	*cup sugar, minus 2 tablespoons*
1	*egg*
1	*cup chopped pecans*

Place apples in a 9" round cake pan. Mix together with cinnamon, sugar and lemon juice. In a saucepan, melt butter. Remove from heat and add flour, sugar, egg and pecans. Pour this mixture evenly over apples and bake at 350° for 45–55 minutes. Let cool slightly, serve warm with vanilla ice cream.

Yield: one 9-inch cake

FOOD PROCESSOR METHOD

With the slicing disc in place, slice apples, using moderate pressure. Place apples into baking dish and mix together with cinnamon, sugar and lemon juice. With steel knife in place, add flour, sugar and nuts to work bowl. Process on and off to chop nuts. Add melted butter and egg to bowl, and process on and off, just until flour disappears. Pour over apples, and follow baking directions.

CARROT CAKE

1 1/2	cup vegetable oil
2	cups sugar
3	eggs
2	teaspoons vanilla
2	cups grated carrots
1	can (8 1/4 ounce) can of crushed pineapple (do not drain)
1/2	cup chopped nuts
3	cups all-purpose flour
2	teaspoons baking soda
1/2	teaspoon salt
1	tablespoon cinnamon

In large bowl, beat together oil, sugar, eggs and vanilla. Add carrots, pineapple and nuts. Blend in flour, soda, salt and cinnamon. Pour into greased and floured 13" x 9" baking dish. Bake at 350° for 30–40 minutes. Cool cake thoroughly. Frost when completely cooled.

CREAM CHEESE FROSTING

1	package (8 ounce) cream cheese
1/4	cup butter or margarine
1	pound box powdered sugar
1/2	teaspoon lemon extract
1	teaspoon vanilla extract

In a large bowl, beat together cream cheese and butter. Add powdered sugar and extracts and beat until smooth and of spreading consistency.

FOOD PROCESSOR METHOD

With shredding disc in place, grate carrots and set aside. With steel knife in place, process oil, sugar, eggs and vanilla. Add carrots, pineapple and nuts and process on and off 2–3 times. Add flour, soda, salt and cinnamon and process on and off until flour disappears. Pour into prepared pan and bake as directed.

Frosting: Place cream cheese, extracts and butter in work bowl with steel knife in place. Process until smooth. Add powdered sugar and process until smooth. Frost thoroughly cooled cake.

BLUEBERRY CRUMB COFFEECAKE

CRUMB TOPPING

1/3   *cup sugar*
6   *tablespoons butter*
3/4   *cup flour*

CAKE

1/2   *cup butter*
1   *cup sugar*
2   *eggs*
1   *cup sifted flour*
1   *teaspoon baking powder*
1   *cup fresh or frozen blueberries*

In small bowl, prepare topping. Cut butter into flour and sugar, until it resembles coarse meal. Set aside.

In large bowl, cream butter and add sugar. Add eggs one at a time and blend in. Stir in flour and baking powder. Gently fold in blueberries, Pour into a greased and floured 8" square pan. Top cake batter with crumb topping and bake at 350° for 45 minutes.

Yield: 8 servings

FOOD PROCESSOR METHOD

With steel knife in place, prepare crumb topping by cutting butter into 1/2 inch pieces. Drop butter onto flour and sugar in work bowl. Set this mixture aside in a small bowl. Using same work bowl and steel knife, process sugar and eggs until well blended. Add butter and process until smooth. Add flour and baking powder and pulse on and off until flour just disappears. Remove steel knife and gently fold blueberries into batter. Pour into prepared pan and top with crumb topping. Bake as directed.

CINNAMON PULL-APART COFFEE CAKE

1	*package active dry yeast*
1/2	*cup warm milk*
1/4	*cup sugar*
1/2	*cup butter*
3	*cups all-purpose flour*
1/2	*teaspoon salt*
2	*eggs*
1/2	*cup melted butter*
1/2	*cup sugar mixed with 1 teaspoon cinnamon*

Combine yeast with warm milk, sugar and butter. Set aside for 5–8 minutes. In large bowl, combine flour and salt, add yeast mixture and eggs, blending until smooth. Turn out onto a floured board and knead until smooth and elastic. Place in a greased bowl for 1 1/2 hours, or until dough has doubled in bulk.

Punch dough down, and let rise again for 45 minutes. Punch dough down, then break off 1 inch pieces of dough. Dip them into melted butter and roll in cinnamon and sugar.

Place in a greased 8" round cake pan, or a cast iron skillet. Let rise for 30 minutes. Bake at 350° for 25–30 minutes. Sift confectioner's sugar over top and serve warm.

Yield: 6–8 servings

FOOD PROCESSOR METHOD

Proof yeast with sugar, warm milk and butter. With steel knife in place, add flour and salt to work bowl. With machine running add yeast mixture and eggs. Let the machine run until dough forms a smooth ball. Turn into greased bowl and let rise, following rising and baking instructions above.

Artichoke Bread Appetizer

1	stick butter or margarine
6	cloves garlic, crushed
4	cups french bread cut into 1/2" cubes
1 1/2	cups sour cream
1	cup grated mozzarella cheese
1/2	cup grated parmesan cheese
1	medium tomato, sliced into 1/2" slices
1/2	cup black olives
1/4	cup grated cheddar cheese
1	package frozen artichoke hearts, defrosted, drained and chopped

In a skillet, melt butter, add garlic and sauté over medium heat, until garlic is translucent and not brown. Remove from heat, add bread cubes, and coat with butter.

In large bowl, combine sour cream, mozzarella and parmesan cheese. Add bread cubes and artichoke hearts. Spread mixture into 8" square or round pan and bake at 350° for 20 minutes.

Remove from oven and top with sliced tomatoes, black olives and additional grated cheddar cheese. Return to oven for 10 minutes or until cheese is melted. Remove from oven. Let stand 5 minutes, cut into squares and serve as an appetizer or bread.

Yield: 8–10 servings

SOUTHERN CORN BREAD

This corn bread is traditionally made in a cast iron skillet, but can be made in a 9" round or square pan.

> 1   *egg*
> 1   *cup buttermilk*
> 1   *cup yellow corn meal*
> 1   *teaspoon sugar*
> 1/2   *teaspoon salt*
> 1   *tablespoon melted bacon drippings*
> 1/2   *teaspoon baking soda*
> 1   *teaspoon baking powder*
> 1   *tablespoon water*

Break egg into buttermilk and beat well. Add corn meal, sugar, salt and drippings. Mix soda and baking powder in water, add to batter. Pour into hot greased iron skillet (or baking pan), bake at 450° for 20 minutes.

Yield: 6–8 servings

FOOD PROCESSOR METHOD

With steel knife in place, process egg, buttermilk, sugar, salt and drippings. Mix soda and baking powder in water, add to work bowl and process on and off 2–3 times. Add corn meal and process until corn meal disappears. Pour into prepared pan and bake as directed.